M000099832

SCHNOODLE AND SCHNOODLES

Your Perfect Schnoodle Guide

Includes Schnoodle Puppies, Giant Schnoodles, Finding
Schnoodle Breeders, Temperament, Miniature Schnoodles,
Care, And More!

By Susanne Saben
© DYM Worldwide Publishers

DYM Worldwide Publishers

ISBN: 978-1-911355-12-0

covered. The information included in this book has been compiled to give an overview of the subject matter covered. The information contained in this book has been compiled to provide an overview of the subject. It is not intended as medical advice and should not be construed as such. For a firm diagnosis of any medical conditions you should consult a doctor or veterinarian (as related to animal health). The writer, publisher, distributors, and/or affiliates of this work are not responsible for any damages or negative consequences following any of the treatments or methods highlighted in this book. Website links are for informational purposes only and should not be seen as a personal endorsement; the same applies to any products or services mentioned in this work. The reader should also be aware that although the web links included were correct at the time of writing they may become out of date in the future. Any pricing or currency exchange rate information was correct at the time of writing but may become out of date in the future. The Author, Publisher, distributors, and/or affiliates assume no responsibility for pricing and currency exchange rates mentioned within this work.

Table of Contents

* * *

Foreword

Like many dog lovers, I enjoy learning and reading about as many different breeds as I possibly can. No two dog breeds are alike, just like no two dogs within that breed are exactly alike. I especially love it when I discover a breed that I didn't know about before, and believe it or not; new breeds are emerging all the time. However, beyond the kennel club recognized 'purebreds,' there's another sort of dog entirely: designer breeds.

Designer dogs are dogs whose parents are two different (usually purebred) breeds. For a very long time such dogs were simply lumped in with other 'mutts' or 'mongrels', but designer breeds are different. The parents are carefully selected for their temperament, physical features, and health, resulting in a mixed-breed dog that, in many people's opinion, is superior to the original breeds used to create them.

The first known example of a purposely bred designer dog was the Labradoodle. In the 1970's, a breeder had the idea to cross a Labrador with a Standard Poodle in order to create a hypoallergenic service dog. But the Labradoodle's popularity didn't stop there; within a few short years, the Labradoodle craze had taken over the Western world. To this day, it remains one of the most sought-after dogs in the world.

Many dog breeders seized the opportunity to draw on the Labradoodle's fame, and soon after the Labradoodle's arrival into mainstream society, dozens upon dozens of designer mixes were created; Maltipoos, Puggles,

Cockapoos, Pomskies, Chorkies—the list goes on and on! There are literally hundreds of possible combinations, and new designer breeds are being introduced all the time.

However, in this book, we will focus on one—the Schnoodle.

I owned a beautiful female Schnoodle named Polly. I took her in after her previous owner passed away, and Polly stole my heart right away. She had a jet-black, slightly curly coat and expressive eyes, and she was as gentle as she was intelligent and loyal. She would wait patiently beside the door for me to come home every evening, then leap around my feet, barking with joy.

She passed away five years ago, and I still mourn for Polly. She was an incredible dog, and although purebred enthusiasts might turn up their nose at designer breeds, I've harbored a deep love for Schnoodles ever since.

Schnoodles are, as the name suggests, a cross between a Schnauzer and a Poodle. It is one of the most popular hybrid breeds, due to its easygoing nature, friendly temperament, and high intelligence.

Schnoodles are, for the most part, very easy to train (a genetic gift from the Poodle, whose intelligence and trainability has made it a favorite amongst dog owners for hundreds of years). Despite having a long coat, they don't shed much and are hypoallergenic, like their Poodle parents. Their slightly curly hair comes in a wide variety of colors— white, black, gray, silver, tan, apricot, gold, and every shade in between!

Foreword

The size of a Schnoodle really depends on its parents; there are many different size variations of both the Poodle and the Schnauzer. A Schnoodle whose parents are a Giant Schnauzer and a Standard Poodle will be a large dog, while a Schnoodle bred from a Miniature Schnauzer and a Toy Poodle will usually be very small. Most Schnoodles are bred from miniature parents, meaning they will be small.

Although this designer breed is relatively low-maintenance and easy to take care of, there are still many things you should know before you get one, to ensure that both you and the Schnoodle are suited for each other. There are unique challenges to owning and caring for a Schnoodle, and we'll cover them all in this book.

My undying love for Schnoodles, and for all dogs in general, inspired me to write this guide, filled with information, do's and don'ts, and tips to properly care for this unique, incredible dog.

Without further ado, thank you very much for reading, and I do hope that you enjoy this book!

Chapter 1 – Schnoodles – What Are They?

One of the absolute best things about the Schnoodle is that it combines the most prominent—and, in my opinion, the most adorable—features of each breed all together in one furry package. The Schnauzer is known for its bearded snout and stocky body, and the Poodle is famous for its dense, slightly curly, non-shedding coat. When combined, the result is a dog with a strong, powerful body and delicate facial features— a unique, endearing combination!

In this chapter, we'll cover some of the basic attributes of the Schnoodle, such as size, coat length and color, and temperament.

Schnauzer-Poodle Mix – Size Variations

As stated in the introduction, the size of a Schnoodle can vary greatly depending on the size of its parents. Now, however, we'll go into greater detail.

First off, there are three different varieties each of Poodles and Schnauzers; Toy, Miniature, and Standard Poodles, and Miniature, Standard, and Giant Schnauzers. Depending on the combination of the parents' sizes, a Schnoodle can range from anywhere from five pounds (2.2 kilograms) all the way up to a hundred pounds (45.3 kilograms)!

Polly, the Schnoodle that I owned years ago, was a Miniature Schnoodle who tipped the scales at just over eight pounds (3.6 kilograms). However, her previous owner, who was a family friend, bought Polly as a puppy from an anonymous breeder who insisted that she would grow much larger. My friend bought all sorts of items for her new puppy, like a large collar and enormous chew toys, that Polly never grew into!

My point is, it's incredibly important to know the sizes of your Schnoodle's parents before you bring him home if you're getting a puppy. I'm sure it would definitely be an unpleasant surprise if the pup you think is a Miniature Schnoodle grows into a huge dog! If the breeder is reluctant to let you see your Schnoodle's parents, find another breeder.

The Poodle is one of the most popular dogs in the world! Schnoodles inherit the Poodle's curly coat, remarkably high intelligence, and easygoing nature.

For the most part, Schnauzers and Poodles are bred within

their weight classes (Miniature Schnauzer with Toy Poodle, etc.), creating three different types of Schnoodles; Miniature, Standard, and Giant. All these terms, which refer to different sizes within each breed, can get a little confusing (there's a huge difference between a Standard Poodle and a Standard Schnauzer, after all) but don't worry, we'll break them all down.

Miniature Schnoodle

The Miniature Schnoodle is the smallest breed variant and the most common type of Schnoodle. It is created by breeding a Miniature Schnauzer with a Toy Poodle. This tiny, energetic, adorable Schnoodle can weigh anywhere from 5 to 15 pounds (2.2 to 6.8 kilograms) when fully grown and will stand up to 15 inches (38 centimeters) at the withers.

Standard Schnoodle

The Standard Schnoodle, or the medium-sized Schnoodle, is a cross between the Miniature Poodle and the Standard Schnauzer. It's more energetic than the Miniature Schnoodle, which is more suited to indoor and apartment living than its larger counterpart. When it reaches adulthood, it will stand about 15 to 20 inches (38 to 63 centimeters) at the withers and will weigh anywhere from 20 to 50 pounds (9 to 18 kilograms).

(Note: As with most dog breeds, males tend to be bigger than females; therefore, if you're looking for a slightly smaller Schnoodle, I would recommend choosing a female dog)

Giant Schnoodle

The largest of the Schnoodles, a Giant Schnoodle is a cross between a Standard Poodle and a Giant Schnauzer. True to its name, Giant Schnoodles can get very big! This type of Schnoodle can stand up to 30 inches (76 centimeters) in height, and can weigh up to a hundred pounds (45.3 kilograms). If you choose a Giant Schnoodle, be prepared to care for it as you would any large dog; exercise it every day, provide it with plenty of space to run around, and prepare to feed it lots of food!

Despite their enormous size, Giant Schnoodles are just as loyal and intelligent as their smaller variants, although they do tend to be a bit more stubborn. If you keep a firm handle on his training, however, you'll find that the Giant Schnoodle is just as eager to please and full of love to give as any small dog.

Remember, because Schnoodles are not purebreds, there is no 'breed standard.' No two Schnoodles are exactly the same; they come in such a wide array of colors, sizes, and body types. Of course, this is one of the many wonderful things about Schnoodles—every dog is unique!

The Coat of The Poodle Schnauzer Mix

The most notable feature of the Schnoodle is its coat. Both the Poodle and the Schnauzer have a medium-length coat; however, the texture of the coat is different. Your Schnoodle may sport the soft, slightly curly hair of the Poodle, or the wiry, rougher coat of the Schnauzer, depending on its genes.

No matter the texture, however, Schnoodles are hypoallergenic, meaning that they produce little to no dander. Doggy dander is what triggers allergic reactions in people who are allergic to dogs, which means that Schnoodles, along with a few other breeds, are the perfect choice for people who want to own a dog but can't hold one for more than a few minutes without sneezing!

The dignified, striking appearance of the Schnauzer is not lost in the Schnoodle! Schnoodles inherit the Schnauzer's 'bearded' look as well as its stocky body structure.

Additionally, the coat of the Schnoodle is much easier to take care of than many other long-coated dogs, like the Pomeranian and Maltese. While grooming is required, Schnoodles shed very little and usually don't require daily brushing.

However, weekly brushings are still recommended to keep his hair and skin clean and healthy. The hair around his eyes and ears will need to be kept trimmed, to prevent painful infections. We'll cover that more in depth in the Grooming chapter. However, if you're looking for a dog with a relatively low-maintenance coat, the Schnoodle might just be right for you!

Apricot Schnoodle, Black Schnoodle, Chocolate Schnoodle - What Causes the Coat Color?

The Schnoodle comes in a virtual rainbow of colors! A single litter of Schnoodles can produce dogs that have different-colored coats; and once again, this is thanks to the Poodle's genes.

While Schnauzers typically only have black or, rarely, brown coats, the Poodle's coat can be almost any color imaginable.

Black Schnoodles, Apricot Schnoodles, and Chocolate Schnoodles are just some of the color variations found in this designer breed—tan, silver, charcoal, and white are also common. While your Schnoodle will most likely be one solid color, different-colored patterns are also likely. Black-and-Tan Schnoodles are not unheard of, although they are rarer than other varieties.

General Anatomy of the Poodle Schnauzer Mix

The Schnoodle is one of the more unusual-looking designer breeds; and, in my humble opinion, one of the most handsome ones as well.

The adorable Schnoodle has several key characteristics that set it apart from the crowd and make it rather easy to identify.

Ideally, the Schnoodle should have a round head with almond-shaped eyes.

The ears should also be uncropped. Floppy ears are crucial to the signature look of the Schnoodle, and cropping them (a process in which a dog's ear flaps are removed when they are still puppies) is both unnecessary and cruel.

Although the Schnoodle's hair will mostly be medium-length, the hair around his eyes and ears will usually grow longer, creating a charming 'bearded' effect. This, combined with its short muzzle and stocky body, gives it a very distinctive look.

The Best Environment For A Schnoodle

When selecting a dog, it's always an excellent, and perhaps necessary, idea to appraise your house, family, and neighborhood, then choose a dog best suited to your environment. For example, a Great Dane isn't the best choice for you if you live in an apartment or flat, and a tiny little Chihuahua won't need a huge yard to run around in. Luckily, Schnoodles are extremely adaptable dogs.

When compared to other dogs of its size, all varieties of Schnoodles are much calmer. The smaller versions are best adapted to apartment life. They don't need as much exercise as terriers or hounds; be sure to take them for short daily walks. However, some Schnoodles tend to be noisy barkers, so if you live in an apartment, you should prepare to train your Schnoodle not to bark unnecessarily (your neighbors, not to mention your landlord, will definitely thank you!). If you're interested in acquiring a Giant Schnoodle, they will, of course, need more exercise than a Miniature or Standard Schnoodle. While they can adapt to apartment living, a house with a large fenced-in yard is the best choice.

Schnoodles are happy, friendly dogs that love being around people! They are gentle and aren't inherently aggressive, making them a perfect choice for large families and families with young children, although they are equally happy with couples and single people—just be sure to give your Schnoodle plenty of love and attention no matter what the size of your family.

Schnoodle Temperament

Designer dogs are beautiful and unique creatures. Unfortunately, the fact of the matter is that many designer dogs were bred for their looks alone, and temperament (the most important thing you should consider before you get ANY dog) was often overlooked in the breeding process. The result is that some designer dogs, while cute, simply don't make good pets for everyone. They might be inherently aggressive, aloof, or hard to train, resulting in their owners abandoning them or surrendering them to animal shelters.

I've been a part-time volunteer at my local animal shelter for many years now, and I've lost count of the number of designer dogs that I've seen walk through these doors, simply because the owners were unaware of the temperament of the dog's parents, and selected a dog with an undesirable disposition.

However, I'm pleased to say that this isn't the case with the Schnoodle. Schnoodles, as I previously stated, are bred from Schnauzers and Poodles—both gentle, intelligent, friendly dogs, resulting in a remarkably well-tempered pet!

Schnoodles are extremely friendly towards their family members, and depending on your Schnoodle's unique individual personality, sometimes strangers as well. But some Schnoodles are more aloof than others towards people that they are unfamiliar with, so you should also keep that in mind if you plan on owning a Schnoodle.

Schnoodles love children. Although they are calm dogs by nature, they still love to play, and they are gentle with children, making them a fantastic choice for anyone who might be worried about introducing a dog to their children. However, even though they are gentle dogs, it's still recommended always to supervise dogs and children, no matter the breed of the dog or the age of the child.

The History of the Schnoodle

Unfortunately, there isn't much available information regarding the history of the Schnoodle, as this designer breed is relatively new.

In the past, Schnauzers were often crossbred with various terrier breeds in England, both to serve as companions and to sniff out valuable truffles. The first intentional breeding between a Schnauzer and a Poodle in the United States occurred in Minnesota in the 1980's. Within just a few years, Schnoodle puppies became more and more common. While Schnoodles aren't the most well-known of the designer breeds, they've attracted a dedicated and loyal following, and there are many die-hard fans of the Schnoodle today. In fact, several celebrities have owned Schnoodles, including Dakota Fanning and Natalie Portman!

It's not surprising that the Schnoodle's grace and charm has attracted fans!

The main motive for crossing Poodles with other breeds is to create a hypoallergenic dog; thus, it only made sense to cross the Poodle with another low-dander dog, the Schnauzer.

The Schnoodle is so new that not all breed associations will recognize it. The American, United, and Canadian Kennel Clubs do not officially recognize the Schnoodle, as it is a 'hybrid breed.' Additionally, most if not all official kennel clubs will not accept Schnoodles, or any other designer dog, into their databases.

However, there are other associations that recognize the Schnoodle as a valid sub-breed—the American Canine Hybrid Club, Designer Dogs Kennel Club, and the Dog Registry of America are organizations that focus on the wide variety of hybrid and designer dogs.

Despite the fact that Schnoodles are a new hybrid breed and the fact that there are no set breed standards, I am fully confident that the Schnoodle, with its easygoing nature, gorgeous appearance, and outstanding temperament, is definitely here to stay!

Intelligence, friendliness, and playfulness—
the Schnoodle certainly is the best of all worlds!

Chapter 2 – Schnoodle Puppies – What to Expect Before Buying One

There are few joys in life greater than bringing home a new puppy. Puppies are so enthusiastic and full of love to give. And, it's an absolute joy watching them grow to their full potential, helping them along the path to adulthood. Schnoodle puppies are some of the cutest that you could find anywhere; however, before you make the decision to bring one into your life, there' are several key things that you should keep in mind.

Schnoodle Cost

Like all puppies, the cost of buying a Schnoodle puppy truly is dependent on where you go and where you look.

Schnoodle Breeders Are the Most Expensive

The most popular choice for people looking for purebred or designer dogs, breeders are people who breed dogs and sell the puppies for profit. Choosing a breeder certainly has its upsides; you know exactly where your puppy came from and that its bloodline is pure.

However, not all breeders are the same, and many are borderline unethical and negligent in the care of their dogs. It's extremely important to research the breeder thoroughly before you buy a puppy from them.

Things that you should watch out for while dealing with a dog breeder:

- A reluctance to let you tour the facilities or to allow you to meet the puppy's parents—this usually means that they keep their dogs in unsanitary or dangerous conditions, or that the puppy they're attempting to sell to you isn't the breed that they're labeled as. For instance, my old Schnoodle, Polly, was sold by a man who claimed that she was a Giant Schnoodle, simply so he could charge my poor friend a higher price for a 'rarer' dog. If my friend had been allowed to meet Polly's parents, she would have known right away that Polly was not, in fact, a Giant Schnoodle, but a Miniature one.

- Anonymity. If a breeder refuses to meet you face-to-face and depends on a third party or a shipping service to deliver their puppies, do not buy from them under any circumstances.

- A history of unreliability or fraud. Interview others who have purchased puppies from the same breeder. You can sometimes learn more from fellow buyers than you might think.

Fortunately, for every unethical breeder, there is one that treats their dogs with love, care, and respect.

However, if you are considering buying from a breeder, know this: it is definitely the more expensive choice. Breeders, especially excellent ones with a steady clientele and a good reputation, charge big bucks for their designer puppies. Schnoodle puppies can carry a price tag of up to twelve hundred dollars (£822)! That's incredibly expensive and a lot of money to spend on a puppy, especially if you're on a budget.

If you can afford it, buying from a good breeder is a great choice, and will be worth the peace of mind to know where your dog came from and that he was bred safely and responsibly. If you can't, however, there are two cheaper options that you might want to consider.

Schnoodle puppies are adorable, but they can be costly!

Schnoodles for Adoption Can Cost Less

Fortunately, there are many breed-specific adoption agencies available. These agencies take in lost, abandoned, or neglected dogs of a certain breed (or, in many cases, hybrid breeds) and find good homes for them. There are several Schnoodle adoption agencies and rescue groups, and they're most certainly worth looking into; there might be one in your area. You will have to pay an adoption fee, of course, but it will certainly cost less than what you would pay for a Schnoodle puppy from a breeder. And, you will get the added satisfaction of knowing that your money will go on to support the group in their efforts to rescue and rehome as many abandoned Schnoodles as possible.

However, there is a slight downside. If you rescue a Schnoodle, you might not be able to get much information on the dog's parentage, genetic health risks, temperament, or previous vaccinations. Also, if you're looking for a Schnoodle puppy, you might not be able to find one; it's well-known that most rescue dogs are adults, as sadly many people buy puppies and then surrender them when they become adults. However, if you can adopt a Schnoodle, I highly recommend it; you will make a huge difference in that dog's life.

Another option that's worth some consideration is an animal shelter. Over seven million dogs and cats are surrendered to animal shelters every year. These facilities, which often operate only on donations and the hard work of volunteers, are usually overcrowded with homeless animals.

It's a commonly held misconception that the majority of pets found in animal shelters are sickly, old mixed breed with health problems and undesirable temperaments—and unfortunately, that assumption leads many people to overlook animal shelters in their quest to find the perfect pet.

The truth is, purebreds and designer breeds are just as likely to wind up in an animal shelter as a mixed breed dog. In my time as an animal shelter volunteer, I've seen just as many purebred dogs surrendered to our care as any other type of dog. People surrender their animals to shelters for many different reasons, and, unlike what many people think, these reasons often have absolutely nothing to do with the dog's appearance, health, or behavior. Most shelter dogs are healthy and happy, and only need you to rescue them and give them a safe, loving home.

I've seen many, many Schnoodles pass through my local animal shelter, often surrendered because of a life change in the owner or rescued from horrible puppy mills or irresponsible breeders. Therefore, it wouldn't be a bad idea to check with animal shelters in your area to see if they have any Schnoodles available for adoption. If there are none, don't lose hope. Talk to the volunteers and give them your contact information; they might be willing to contact you first the next time a Schnoodle arrives at the shelter.

The same downsides to adopting from rescue groups and adoption agencies apply here as well.

There's one other low-cost option if you're looking to acquire a Schnoodle: classified ads. Many people will sell, rehome, or give away the dogs that they can no longer care for in newspapers and online classified ads. You will likely pay far less for one of these dogs than you would from a breeder.

A word of caution, however—do not purchase puppies this way. Many puppy mill owners will sell their dogs online or through newspapers to retain anonymity and protect themselves from prosecution (I'll discuss puppy mills in greater detail in later chapters).

Schnoodle Cost—Other Factors

Schnoodles are, thankfully, relatively low-maintenance dogs; however, there are still some costs that can't be avoided. Food, healthcare, toys and accessories, training, and grooming, to name a few, can become costly; however, if you prepare a budget before bringing home a puppy, you can ensure that both your new Schnoodle and your banking account will be comfortable! It's key, however, to understand what exactly your Schnoodle will need and how much it will cost you every month.

First off is food. Nearly everyone is on a budget these days; therefore, it might be tempting to settle for a cheap brand of dog food that you can buy in bulk to cut costs. But, to keep your Schnoodle healthy, you must buy a high-quality dog food that's low on fillers and additives yet high in protein.

High-quality dog food can be quite expensive; however, the smaller varieties of Schnoodles don't eat very much, which sort of balances it out. Bigger Schnoodles, though, eat a lot, which means that if you're on a budget, and if you want to get a Giant or Standard Schnoodle, be sure to set aside enough money to ensure that you can purchase the food that they need.

Thankfully, Schnoodles don't need nearly as much grooming as some other breeds, and they don't shed very much, but the Schnoodle's coat still needs a good brushing on a regular basis, and you will need to bathe your Schnoodle weekly to keep his coat clean. Fortunately, grooming supplies aren't too expensive, and they last a long time, but if you want to get your Schnoodle professionally groomed, you will have to take him every six to eight weeks, which can get expensive.

What Is Your Activity Level?

Before you get a Schnoodle, it's important to evaluate yourself and understand this breed's activity level. Will you be able to provide it with the exercise that it needs?

Miniature Schnoodles are the best type of Schnoodle to have if you live in an apartment, or if you don't have the time or energy to take them on long walks or to dog parks. Since they're so small, they don't need nearly as much exercise as their larger counterparts.

Standard and Giant Schnoodles, however, have more energy that they need to expend. If they don't get enough exercise, they can become restless, agitated, hyper, and destructive — not to mention unhappy. Dogs get bored just as easily as we do, after all!

If you are not active, or you don't have the time to be active, or you aren't physically able to get the dog outside for whatever reason, then you can always hire a dog walker in your area. Dog walkers are fantastic, and an absolute lifesaver for people who have to work and don't have time for a thirty-minute walk every day!

How Many Schnoodles Should You Have?

Schnoodles are relatively calm dogs, but they still love to play! If you're not going to be able to spend as much time with your Schnoodle as you'd like, it would be a good idea to get more than one Schnoodle to keep each other company.

Schnoodles are sociable dogs that get along with others well. They aren't aggressive unless they're mistreated or unhappy, so you won't have to worry about them fighting with each other. The main factor to take into consideration is your money and time. Two Schnoodles are, of course, twice as expensive as one, and will require more time and dedication to their health and wellbeing. Depending on your living situation, you might not be able to own more than one dog. (Many leases have a limit on how many dogs you can have). But if you can, I'd highly recommend getting more than one Schnoodle, especially two from the same litter. The more, the merrier!

Where Do You Live?

As mentioned earlier, the size of a Schnoodle can vary. Most Schnoodles are mid-sized and are suitable for apartment living. However, Giant Schnoodles can be massive! Depending on their genes, they can weigh up to 100 pounds (45.3 kilograms).

Be sure to keep that maximum weight in mind. When selecting a Schnoodle puppy, you should look at its parents so you can see how large they are. You can't always tell how large a Schnoodle puppy will be just by looking at the puppy itself.

With this in mind, you must make sure you choose a Schnoodle that is suitable for your living environment. A larger home is better for a Giant Schnoodle, for instance. A smaller apartment is obviously better for a much smaller version of the dog.

Checklist

Yes	No	
Yes	No	Will I be able to spend enough time with my Schnoodle?
Yes	No	Will I be able to afford the costs associated with caring for my Schnoodle?
Yes	No	Is my home suited for a Schnoodle?
Yes	No	Do I have enough time to exercise my Schnoodle? Do I have lots of space available for my Schnoodle, if he is large and has lots of energy, to run around?
Yes	No	Am I willing to put in the effort to groom my Schnoodle?

If you answered "yes" to all of these questions, then you are ready to open up your heart and your home to a Schnoodle!

Chapter 3 – Schnoodles for Sale—Buying Schnoodle Puppies From a Breeder

This is a subject that I touched upon a bit in the previous chapter. But here, we'll go into greater detail because finding a suitable breeder is an extremely important process.

It's an exciting journey, looking for the perfect Schnoodle puppy to add to your family. However, you also must be extremely cautious in your search for a breeder. Dog breeding is a practice that, in many parts of the world, isn't regulated—meaning that practically anyone can breed and sell dogs. Because of this, it's crucial to find a breeder that is both professional and compassionate about the animals that they breed.

A good breeder can be an invaluable part of you and your Schnoodle's life. Many breeders offer services that go far beyond simply selling you a puppy, and it would be a good idea to build a lasting relationship with your Schnoodle's breeder.

In this chapter, we'll discuss how to find a Schnoodle breeder, how a breeder cares for his or her puppies, how to choose an ethical breeder, and the dangers of backyard breeders and puppy mills.

What Can Schnoodle Breeders Do For You?

Thanks to the explosion in the popularity of designer breeds, there are hundreds of breeders out there who specialize in breeding designer dogs. However, finding a Schnoodle puppy isn't as easy as finding, say, a Golden Retriever. You have to do your research, and that may mean traveling a long way to find a breeder. But don't give up in your search! A great Schnoodle breeder can make the puppy-buying experience much easier and less stressful for everyone involved.

There are two types of Schnoodle breeders; people who breed Poodles and Schnauzers together to create first-generation Schnoodle puppies to sell, and people who breed multi-generational Schnoodles. That is to say, breeding one Schnoodle with another. Either way, a great breeder will be extremely knowledgeable about Schnoodles as well as the parent breeds. Be sure to ask many questions! If your breeder can answer them correctly, that's definitely a good sign.

All Schnoodles deserve to be treated with love and respect. Always make sure that you buy puppies from a responsible breeder.

A great breeder won't simply breed two dogs together and sell the puppies. Someone who's passionate about the Schnoodles that they breed, and who genuinely cares about the health and safety of their dogs, will work hard to do the following:

- Ensure that the puppy's parents are healthy and receive regular vet care.

- Follow ethical breeding practices. A female dog, no matter the breed, should not be bred on her first or second heat cycle, and should be allowed to wait until after another full heat cycle before breeding again. It's dangerous to the mother's health to be bred continuously. Be sure to ask the breeder how many litters the mother has had and how often she is bred.

- Provide adequate food, water, shelter, grooming, and vet care to all of their dogs.

- Provide proof of vaccination. Since the breeder is responsible for the puppies during the earliest, most vulnerable stages of their life, he or she should ensure that the puppies are vaccinated against some of the many life-threatening diseases that puppies are prone to. Always ask for complete documentation and, if you'd like to take the extra step for peace of mind, the contact information of the veterinarian who administered the vaccines.

Can Schnauzer or Poodle Breeders Work?

Did I mention that the Schnoodle is a relatively new designer breed?

Because of how rare Schnoodles are, there aren't a ton of good, reputable breeders that breed and sell Schnoodles, and often these breeders sell puppies before they're even born. You might have to be put on a waiting list, meaning you might have to wait up to a year or more to get your Schnoodle puppy.

However, never fear—there's another option you can look into, and with any luck, you'll be able to bring your new best friend home much sooner!

If you're unable to find a Schnoodle puppy from a good, responsible breeder, you can try contacting a Schnauzer or Poodle breeder. Explain your situation, and especially explain why you want a Schnoodle that has been bred responsibly. If they're willing, the breeder might be able to get in contact with another breeder to produce a litter of Schnoodles to sell!

Not all breeders are willing to do this, of course. But since Poodle and Schnauzer breeders are more common than Schnoodle breeders, you just might have an easier time getting a Schnoodle puppy this way.

Also, even if the breeder isn't willing to breed one of their own dogs, they might just be able to refer you to another breeder who will.

What To Ask

Think about the last time you bought a car. I'm sure you asked the salesperson all sorts of questions: how many miles to the gallon does the vehicle get? Was the vehicle was involved in any accidents? How many miles has it been driven? And, what sort of safety features does the car have?

When making such a major purchase, it's only natural and even expected to ask lots of questions!

Buying a dog is no different. I certainly hope that you won't be asked to pay the price of a car for your puppy, but apart from the price, a dog is just as important (more important, in my opinion) than any car. You're not just buying a pet; you're selecting the newest member of your family!

My point being, you should ask the breeder many, many questions before you purchase a puppy.

- Ask about the seller's experience with the Schnoodle breed. It's important to buy from someone who understands how this designer breed behaves, thinks, and develops.

- Ask about the overall demeanor of a dog you're interested in. Look to see if the owner understands and is observant of a particular puppy's personality. Any good breeder pays attention to each individual dog and can tell you how he acts and how his siblings treat him.

- Get details on the bloodline of the pup you're interested in. Are the mother and father healthy? His grandparents? Will your puppy be prone to any genetic health problems?

- Talk about the vaccinations that the dog has received. Ask for availability of papers proving that the dog has gotten necessary vaccinations. A good breeder will be more than willing to give you these details.

Problems To Avoid

In my lifetime, I've encountered, spoken to, and befriended many excellent breeders. I am in no way trying to cast any negative light on dog breeders in general; I have nothing but respect for the people who breed and sell dogs. However, dog breeding is a lucrative industry. It is also unregulated in many parts of the world.

Because of this, puppy mills and unscrupulous backyard breeders are, unfortunately, relatively common. Puppy mills and 'backyard breeders' are essentially the same things; high-demand dogs, like the Schnoodle, are locked in cages or tiny pens, often without adequate food or water, and are forced to breed over and over again. The puppies are sold before they're ready to leave their mother. And, the dogs rarely, if ever, get any medical treatment. The dogs are often starving, sick, and lonely, and once they can no longer breed, they are abandoned or killed.

In my work as an animal shelter volunteer, I've seen the same tragedy in different settings many times over. It's an outrage, and I for one can't understand how some people are capable of that sort of cruelty.

Because people can earn a lot of money breeding dogs, it's never going to go away really unless we, the consumers, are made aware of puppy mills and backyard breeders. When we buy a dog from someone who hasn't made it clear to us that they breed their dogs responsibly, we run the risk of our money supporting an industry that's responsible for thousands of dog deaths every year.

In your search for a breeder, it's crucial to keep an eye out for any red flags that may point to a cruel and neglectful breeder.

- Avoid buying Schnoodles that don't have their vaccination papers available, even if the breeder insists that the dog has been vaccinated. (However, if the breeder did get the puppy vaccinated but simply doesn't have his records, you can double-check with the veterinarian; however, this is still sort of a red flag, as any professional breeder will keep track of the dogs' documents). Not only will papers ensure that the puppy is up to date on his shots, but they also prove that the breeder really cares about the health and safety of his or her dogs.

- Look to see that the Schnoodle puppy has been properly groomed and that it does not appear to be in any harm or distress.

- Always, ALWAYS avoid buying from any breeder that is reluctant about letting you visit the facilities—someone who will insist on delivering the puppy to you or meeting you somewhere for your convenience. Don't be fooled. More than likely that is a sign that the breeder doesn't want you to see the place that the puppy was born, bred, and housed, nor the condition of the other dogs.

- Never buy a puppy from a breeder who offers 'discounted' dogs or dogs with a 'limited health guarantee'. No ethical breeder would ever sell such puppies because most of the time these dogs are sick. A good breeder puts his or her dog's health and wellbeing above profits. You want to pick a breeder who sees his or her dogs as individuals with wants and needs, not livestock.

- Examine the puppy for signs of malnutrition. A good breeder will always feed his or her dogs high-quality dog food, and feed them the proper amount. People who simply breed dogs for profit often feed their dogs extremely low-quality supermarket food and skip meals to save money. If the Schnoodle puppy is thin, has a dull coat, or seems listless, do not buy from that breeder.

Pet stores

You might notice that I didn't cover pet stores when discussing methods to buy Schnoodles. I didn't forget; I left pet stores out on purpose.

Please, please never buy a Schnoodle puppy from a pet store. It is estimated that ninety-nine percent of all puppies sold at pet stores come from puppy mills. Pet store owners buy puppies from puppy mills to resell for two reasons— since puppy mills breed female dogs on every heat cycle, puppy mills can provide a steady stream of puppies, and puppies from puppy mills are usually cheaper than puppies from breeders.

Sometimes the people who own pet stores will insist that their puppies come from 'breeders', but since 'breeders' is an arbitrary term, usually this is simply an attempt to trick buyers into thinking that the puppies come from good breeders instead of awful puppy mills.

Chapter 4 –Schnoodle Temperament, Personality, and Intelligence

I've always said owning a dog can bring more joy to a family than almost anything else in the world. Dogs are loving, loyal, incredibly intelligent creatures who only want your love and attention. It's no wonder that millions of people all over the world own dogs!

However, this is a mixed blessing. Many people get dogs without truly researching the breed. Every breed of dog is different and requires different sorts of care. Unfortunately, this often ends in tragedy—dogs abandoned or given up by the people who took them into their homes in the first place.

Owning a dog is not a matter to be taken lightly. You are responsible for not only caring for your dog, but for loving him unconditionally, for he will do the same for you.

There's good news. However, Schnoodles are relatively easy dogs to care for. They're gentle, intelligent, and loyal— perfect for first-time dog owners, families with children, single people, and just about anyone willing to open up their hearts and their homes to one of these shaggy, gorgeous dogs!

Schnoodle Intelligence

One of the Schnoodle's best traits is its intelligence. The Schnoodle is an incredibly smart dog, which makes it easy to train.

Who says that dogs can't be both cute and smart?

The Schnoodle is so smart because it is bred from two of the most intelligent dog breeds in the world: the Schnauzer and the Poodle.

In Stanley Coren's famed book, *The Intelligence of Dogs*, the author gathered information and performed tests to rank different breeds of dogs regarding their intelligence. Over time, Mr. Coren's findings became more or less commonly accepted by most breeders, trainers, and dog enthusiasts as a viable tool to measure dog intelligence.

The author used three different aspects of dog intelligence to create his list.

- The instinctive intelligence of the dog, this refers to how well a dog can herd, guard, be a loyal companion, protect a family, or do other things that it was bred to do.

- Adaptive intelligence; or how well it can solve problems on its own.

- Working or obedience intelligence. How a dog can learn new things from human trainers or owners.

Eighty dog breeds were tested based on those points. Out of all eighty breeds, the two breeds that the Schnoodle is bred from placed very high on the list of the smartest dogs in the world!

The Poodle was ranked in second place, just behind the Border Collie. While the Schnauzer didn't do quite so well, it still ranked very high—the Miniature, Standard and Giant Schnauzers are respectively listed at the 12th, 18th and 28th places on the listing.

Intelligence in dogs, like in people, is usually hereditary, meaning that Schnoodles are excellent or above-average regarding how they can handle new commands or how they can solve problems.

What Is a Schnoodle Like When Compared To the Schnauzer and Poodle?

There are many good characteristics that Schnoodles share with the Schnauzer and Poodle. Of course, every individual Schnoodle will have a different and unique personality. You might find that your Schnoodle is more headstrong, aloof, or playful than the 'breed standard.' This is just a generalization, and it's important to keep in mind that no two Schnoodles are alike, just like no two people are alike. With that being said, however, there are many personality traits that Schnoodles are prone to.

Similarities To The Schnauzer

- The Schnoodle is known for its loyalty to its master, which it inherits from the Schnauzer, which was bred for unwavering loyalty.

- The Schnoodle is also very protective of its owners, particularly children.

- The dog may also be rather independent at times, particularly Schnoodles that are bred from the Giant Schnauzer, but with the right training will still recognize you as the head of the pack.

Similarities To The Poodle

- Poodles are well-known for their playfulness. This is definitely a trait that carries on in the Schnoodle. Prepare for lots of games of fetch and tug-of-war!

- Like its parent breed, the Schnoodle is incredibly intelligent.

- Schnoodles are also very affectionate and friendly.

- Poodles were originally bred as hunting dogs; more specifically, to retrieve waterfowl and bring the carcass back to their masters. Schnoodles might not have the same water-resistant coat as Poodles, but their love for sport and their agility lives on in the Schnoodle.

Remember, always talk to the breeder or the person who previously owned the dog to get a good idea of his personality before you bring him home.

Schnoodle Training – Is the Dog Responsive To Commands?

In dogs, high intelligence doesn't always mean the dog is easy to train. Some of the dogs at the bottom of Mr. Coren's list are smart; they are simply headstrong and independent and do not take commands from people easily.

Fortunately, that is not the case with the Schnoodle. These dogs are smart and eager to please, making them relatively easy to train.

While training your Schnoodle, you have to be as consistent and patient as possible. Your Schnoodle won't listen to you if you get frustrated or take a half-hearted approach to his training. Consistency with proper motivation are keys!

We've all heard the phrase "You can't teach an old dog new tricks." While this certainly isn't true, it *is* true that puppies and young dogs are easier to train than older dogs, which tend to be more set in their ways. If you can, begin your Schnoodle's training when he is between four to eight months in age. The younger the dog is, the easier it will be for him to retain information.

Are Schnoodles Good With People?

Oh, boy. We've all seen it; dogs barking and showing their teeth around new people, maybe even attempting to bite them. Unfortunately, many breeds of dogs are prone to aggression, aloof behavior, and mistrust towards people. Good news--you won't have to worry about that with the Schnoodle! Schnoodles love people, and although some of them might be a bit standoffish towards strangers, they tend to warm up quickly and be willing to greet that person with a friendly wag of the tail.

There's one trait that the Schnoodle may inherit from the Schnauzer, and this is a tendency to become more attached to one person in the family more than the others. My Schnoodle, Polly, would follow me around the house, wagging her tail as fast as she could, and whenever I would sit down, Polly would immediately jump in my lap! She loved me to pieces. She loved my husband and children also, of course, but she tended to go to me for affection before she would go to them. I feel that she and I had a special bond.

My point is, although not all Schnoodles are this way, it's an important point to keep in mind before you get your Schnoodle—more on that in a moment.

Avoiding Problems With Your Schnoodle

Overall, the Schnoodle is a fantastic dog with a wonderful temperament and a loving personality. But like all dogs, there are some steps you should take to negate any negative behaviors that are common in Schnoodles. Some of these behaviors and tendencies were discussed at some length already, but we'll go into a bit more detail about them.

First off, the Schnoodle, while loving towards the entire family, can become attached to one person more than everyone else in the household. While this might not seem like a big deal, it can be. One reason, out of many, that people surrender their dogs to animal shelters is jealousy amongst the family. I've seen it countless times. One memorable incident involved a dejected-looking man who arrived early one morning at the shelter I volunteer at. He was holding a carrier, and in that carrier was a tiny little Chihuahua. The man told me that he'd gotten the Chihuahua for his wife as a Christmas present. She'd been happy with the dog at first, but as Chihuahuas are famous for being one-person dogs, she soon became angry and jealous when the Chihuahua became more attached to her husband and ignored her. Finally, she forced her husband to surrender the dog to our animal shelter.

This is an extremely common occurrence—aloof dogs driving a wedge in between family members. Thankfully, Schnoodles aren't as prone to this one-person behavior as other breeds, but it does happen. To avoid hurt feelings and bickering, it's crucial to involve the entire family in the feeding, walking, playing, and grooming of your Schnoodle, especially while he is still a puppy.

Another common problem with Schnoodles is boredom. This shouldn't come as a surprise; Schnoodles are highly intelligent, athletic dogs. They need daily stimulation, both mental and physical. Otherwise, they become bored, frustrated, and destructive. The last thing you want is to come home to a destroyed house!

Fortunately, all you have to do is provide your Schnoodle with adequate entertainment. Giving him toys and letting him run around the yard isn't enough; you need to play with him in a way that requires him to use his brain.

All breeds, even designer breeds, have some negative traits. Fortunately, the ones that come along with the Schnoodle are easily remedied!

Always provide lots of toys for your Schnoodle so that he doesn't become bored!

Chapter 5 – Schnoodle Feeding and Nutritional Needs

Possibly the most important thing you can do for your Schnoodle (other than providing him with a safe, loving home of course!) is to feed him the right type of food.

If you're a first-time dog owner, a trip to the pet store can be extremely confusing. There're aisles and aisles of food, all different varieties, and that come in different forms—canned, dried, and semi-moist. So what food is best for your Schnoodle? Is there even a difference? Food is food, right?

Well, no. Just like we need different types of food depending on our health, age, weight, and energy requirements, so do dogs—especially dogs like the Schnoodle that come in different sizes.

There's also a big difference between the different brands of dog food. No two brands are the same, and simply by switching dog food brands you can see changes in your Schnoodle's appearance and behavior.

One dilemma that many pet owners face is what, and when, to feed their dog. In this chapter, we'll discuss how to pick a high-quality dog food, the difference between the different types of dog foods, how to make homemade dog food, what food to choose for each stage in your Schnoodle's life, how much to feed your Schnoodle (based on his weight), and the foods that are harmful to your Schnoodle's health.

High-Quality Food vs. Low-Quality Food

Just for a moment, imagine eating the same thing day in and day out. More specifically, something boring and with low nutrient density; white bread and plain mashed potatoes, nothing else, every single day. After the first week, how would you feel? How about after a year?

Low-quality food, aka 'supermarket food' is the white bread of the dog food world. Most of the time it barely meets the already shockingly low standards for animal food set by many food regulation organizations. Low-quality food is cheaply made and is virtually tasteless to dogs. Even worse, it contains a high quantity of fillers, such as corn meal, which nutritionally is unnecessary for a dog's health.

It contains no additional vitamins and minerals that are vital to a dog's well-being, even though it might be labeled 'nutritionally balanced'.

Imagine how miserable you would be eating nothing but low-quality food. A good diet is not only vital for good health, but also for morale. I've seen a world of difference in dogs before simply by switching their food.

High-quality dog food is made from only the best ingredients, is low on fillers, and are often packed with vitamins that your Schnoodle needs for healthy growth and development. As a bonus, dogs love the taste!

So how do you choose a good dog food? How do you weed out low-quality food from high-quality food?

First, never shop for your dog's food at a supermarket. Always go to a pet store.

Second, read the list of ingredients carefully. Avoid anything that contains a high amount of fillers such as corn meal.

Unfortunately, high-quality dog food is, of course, more expensive than grocery store brands; this is only to be expected. It might be a steep price to pay, but please don't give in and buy anything less than a high-quality brand of food.

It might be a good idea to consult your vet before you choose a brand of dog food, and you can always ask the pet store manager or clerks for more information when buying dog food. Most of them are well-informed and can direct you to a certain brand of dog food if you're having trouble deciding what to buy.

Schnoodle Feeding – When to Feed?

Just like people, dogs like routine. It's important to establish a feeding schedule for your Schnoodle. Not only will he learn when to expect his food and when to wait patiently to be fed, but it will also serve to regulate his digestive system if he is fed at the same time every day.

For an adult Schnoodle, it is typically best to feed him twice per day; once in the morning and once again at night. Always give him the same amount to avoid drastic changes in body weight and gastrointestinal upsets.

If your Schnoodle is a puppy under the age of six months, you'll need to feed him more often; three meals a day, in the morning, around noon, and at night, will suffice. He's still a baby, after all, and his growing body demands more energy than an adult dog. Make sure that his food is small enough for him to chew and that he has no difficulty eating. Once his milk teeth strengthen, he won't have too much trouble chewing regular dog food, but you should still provide him with a dog food that's specially formulated for puppies, at least until he's six months old.

How Much Should I Feed My Schnoodle?

Unlike most breeds, purebred or designer, there's no set guidelines for feeding a Schnoodle, simply because of the vast variety of sizes. A Miniature Schnoodle is clearly going to require less food than a Giant Schnoodle, for instance. However, you can base the amount of food in each feeding on your individual dog's body weight.

Below you'll find a chart that will show how much you should feed your Schnoodle per day depending on his body weight. This is just a general guide, and it's wise to take other factors into account when feeding him, such as health, age, and activity level.

Weight	Amount of Food (cups)
Up to 10 pounds (4.5 kg)	¼ to ¾ cups
10-25 pounds (4.5-11.3 kg)	¾ to 1 cup
25-50 pounds (11.3-23 kg)	1 to 2 cups
50-75 pounds (23-34 kg)	2 to 2 ½ cups
Over 75 pounds (34 kg and up)	2-4 cups

Nutrition By Age

When selecting a dog food brand for your Schnoodle, evaluate his age and general physical condition. A younger dog will need food with a higher protein content than an older dog to support his growing muscles and organs, and an older dog will need food with a slightly higher content of healthy fats.

Feeding Schnauzer Poodle Mix Puppies

Young puppies typically consume their mothers' milk in the first two months of their lives. Puppies begin the weaning process they are about three to six weeks in age, and by the second month should progress to eating nothing but solid food.

A Schnoodle puppy needs a high-protein diet, and should be fed three times a day. Carefully control his portions so that he doesn't become overweight. Fat puppies are cute, but they're not healthy!

Feeding Senior Schnoodles

Technically speaking, a senior dog is one that is at least seven years of age. An older dog has different nutritional needs than a younger one, as its metabolic functions will change over time.

There are many brands of dog food that are specially formulated for senior dogs. However, there are other vitamin and mineral supplements that you can add to his food to boost his health and ease his transition into old age.

Some of these aren't usually found in dog food and can be purchased via a veterinarian or a pet supply store.

- Gamma-linolenic acid, or GLA, is an omega-6 fatty acid that is vital to hair and skin health. You might want to add this to your dog's diet because while the liver does naturally produce GLA, a senior dog's liver won't be able to produce it as well.

- FOS can be used in your senior dog's food to improve how well digestive bacteria can be formed in the body. This type of bacterium is used to encourage healthy intestinal functions.

- Vitamin E and beta-carotene should also be added as they are antioxidants that boost the performance of the immune system. Unfortunately, like humans, as dogs get older their immune systems tends to weaken, leaving them vulnerable to illness and disease.

Dry and Semi-Moist Food

There are three types of dog food; wet, dry, and semi-moist. Dry food is by far the most common type of food, the type that many, many dog owners choose to feed to their dogs.

Semi-moist food is somewhat common as well, although not as popular as dry food because it's generally more expensive than dry food and comes in small pouches, which is inconvenient for owners with multiple dogs. However, semi-moist and dry dog foods are lumped into the same category.

As long as the food is high-quality and nutritionally balanced, the preference of wet, dry, or semi-moist is up to you and your Schnoodle. Some dogs prefer dry, others wet.

There are some advantages to choosing dry dog food.

- Dry food is good for your Schnoodle's dental health. The crunchy texture helps to clean his teeth and gums, and vets generally recommend dry food for good oral hygiene.

- Dry food is generally higher in carbohydrates than canned dog food. Carbs are good for your Schnoodle's health, as long as it's not eaten in excess.

- Dry food is cheaper than canned dog food, especially if you have a small dog or multiple dogs. A single large bag of dog food can feed a small

Schnoodle for a month or more, as opposed to one can of dog food per day, which can add up fast!

Canned or 'Wet' Food

The second most popular option is canned food, often called wet food. While dry food is a good option, there are several good things about choosing wet food.

- Canned wet food tends to contain more protein and fat on average, making it a good option for older dogs.

- Wet food tends to be low in artificial colors and flavors. Also, thanks to the canning process, it's low in synthetic preservatives as well.

- Wet food is a good option for dogs who have suffered from tooth loss or have other dental problems that make it difficult to chew hard dry dog food.

You must make sure that the canned food you have is stored properly and that you dispose of anything your dog doesn't eat within an hour. It can be easy for any wet food that is left out for far too long to become contaminated with harmful bacteria. Yuck!

Overall, dry and wet foods are good options to consider alike. It is up to you to figure out what you would prefer to give to your dog. Be sure to think about the positive and negative aspects of each option.

Homemade Food

Beyond the traditional three dog food options—wet, dry, and semi-moist—there's a fourth option, one that is slowly creeping back into popularity—homemade food.

For thousands of years, before dog food was ever made commercially, dogs were fed regular human food, a balance of table scraps and fresh meat. Over the past few decades, the practice has fallen out of fashion, and for good reason: dogs should never, ever be fed on table scraps alone. What's good for you isn't necessarily good for your dog, and his nutritional needs will rarely be met.

However, you can feed him human food, if you feed him the right things, and in the right amount! Many people choose to feed their dogs a fresh diet of meat, fruits, and vegetables, and dogs love it. I feed my Schnoodles a homemade diet, and I'm sure I could never convince them to go back to dry dog food!

I highly recommend this option for a variety of reasons, number one being cost. It doesn't cost too much more to feed your dogs a fresh diet than it does to buy commercially prepared dog food, especially if your Schnoodle is small; small dogs don't eat as much.

However, it's important to ensure that the food you give your Schnoodle is safe for canine consumption. This means not only familiarizing yourself with foods that are toxic for dogs, but also recognizing the other dangers. Contrary to everything nursery rhymes have ever taught us, never give your dog a bone; it can splinter, and shards can lodge in the throat or stomach. Make sure that you wash all fruits and vegetables thoroughly before you feed them to your Schnoodle.

The base of your Schnoodle's homemade diet should be meat. Lean beef, chicken, and pork are great choices; you can also choose to add organ meats such as liver and kidneys. However, contrary to popular belief, dogs aren't carnivores; they're omnivores, and although they do mostly need meat, fruits and vegetables are important for healthy function.

Fruits and Vegetables

Fruits and veggies are an important part of your dog's homemade diet. Dogs need more vegetables than fruit and tend to enjoy them more as well.

Not all fruits and vegetables are suitable for your dog; you will learn about these in the next part of this chapter.

It is best to stick with such fruits and vegetables as:

- Apples

- Bananas

- Pears

- Strawberries

- Watermelon

- Asparagus

- Bell peppers

- Carrots

- Lettuce

- Spinach

- Sweet potatoes

- Green beans

These are all great to have provided that you do the following:

- Remove rinds, peels, cores and seeds from any fruits or vegetables you might offer to your dog.

- You can always boil some of the harder items that you want to give to make them softer and therefore a little easier for your dog to consume properly.

- Wash everything that you want to offer beforehand.

- Try and look for options that have not been treated with pesticides and other chemicals as they might still contain some residues from those items. Fortunately, it's easy to find organic fruits and vegetables at your local grocery store.

What Foods Should You Avoid?

There are plenty of foods that you should avoid giving to your dog:

- Fatty meats

- Raisins

- Grapes

- Citrus fruits; these can cause an upset stomach

- All members of the garlic family, including onions and garlic, can damage red blood cells

- Mushrooms

- Rhubarb

- Chocolate

- Dairy products. The Schnoodle does not have the lactase needed to break down lactose

- Nuts (many dogs have nut allergies, and it's a good idea to avoid them all together)

- Yeast dough. This causes excess gas to develop

- Salts and salty items. These can cause sodium poisoning in some cases

All in all, a good diet is the foundation on which your Schnoodle's health lies. Always do your research before you choose a feeding option for your precious Schnoodle, and remember: When in doubt, call your vet!

Chapter 6 – Schnoodle Health

Unfortunately, it's a well-known fact that many breeds of dogs are more prone to certain health problems than others. For instance, Dachshunds are prone to developing slipped discs in their spine, and Chihuahuas often develop a collapsed trachea. It's crucial to research what types of conditions and diseases a particular breed of dog is prone to before you welcome one into your family, to be prepared for a possible future.

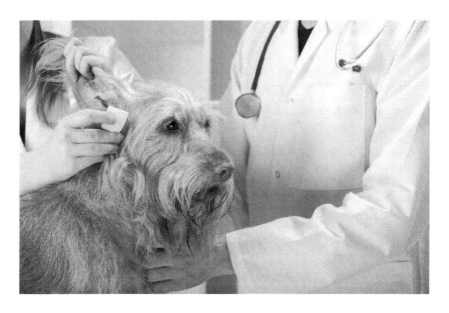

Schnoodles aren't prone to many genetic disorders; however, it's important always to schedule regular vet appointments to make sure he stays healthy.

The good news is that Schnoodles, like many hybrid breeds, are generally healthy. The problem with many purebred dogs is a lack of 'new blood', so to speak, in their gene pools, meaning that inbreeding is extremely common practice, which can lead to all sorts of health problems. With hybrid breeds like the Schnoodle, this isn't as likely; leading to a hardier, robust breed of dog!

However, like all dogs, Schnoodles are susceptible to certain health problems. The most important thing you can do to protect your Schnoodle from potentially fatal diseases is to provide him with consistent vet care.

To fully understand your Schnoodle's health requirements, it's crucial to know as much as you can about their life expectancy, dietary requirements, and illnesses that are common in the breed.

Schnoodle Life Expectancy

Your Schnoodle can live to be about 10 to 15 years on average. This is a relatively long lifespan for a dog.

As a general rule of thumb, smaller dogs usually live longer than large dogs. If you have a Miniature Schnoodle, he will have a better chance of reaching 15 years of age than a Giant Schnoodle. However, with consistent vet care, a good diet, and regular exercise, even a Giant Schnoodle can live a long time.

Why Do Larger Schnoodles Die Younger?

The Giant Schnoodle will be more likely to live for 10 to 12 years on average. In fact, any larger dog is likely to die younger than another dog for a variety of reasons:

- Larger dogs produce high levels of growth hormones. This, in turn, causes them to age quicker.
- The metabolic rates in larger dogs tend to decline faster than smaller dogs as they grow older, leading to obesity—which in turn can cause organ strain, heart disease, and cancer.

- The bones in a larger dog can become weaker over time and more prone to fractures than smaller dogs. A broken bone can lead to infection and the weakening of the immune system.

- Cellular reproduction rates are spread out more in smaller Schnoodles than larger ones. It is easier for a larger dog to grow quickly. This causes the dog's cellular reproduction rate to wear out as they grow older.

The Poodle and Schnauzer Mix Is Very Energetic!

Your Schnoodle will have plenty of energy in its little (or maybe larger) body. You need to give your Schnoodle enough time to exercise and stay active each day. You need to let it run around so it can use up its energy and burn off fats, thus keeping its weight at a healthy level.

Caution: If you do not have a fenced-in yard and live nearby roads, streets, or intersections, do not let your Schnoodle run around outside! They are energetic and inquisitive dogs by nature and therefore run a high risk of being run down by vehicles. Please keep your dog safe and happy; walk him twice a day on a leash. Don't keep him chained up, as

Schnoodles crave company and attention, and he will only be miserable stuck on a chain all day.

You should always give your Schnoodle plenty of toys to play with. Good chew toys and other items that can keep your dog active will certainly help it to expend its energy. Of course, it also helps to keep him from tearing up stuff in your home out of sheer boredom! Just make sure whatever toys you give him are safe for dogs; avoid rawhide and stuffed animals intended for children. Rawhide can be very harmful to smaller dogs, and stuffed animals have small pieces, like plastic eyes and synthetic filling, which can be swallowed.

Walking Your Schnoodle

As mentioned earlier, walking is a great way to expend your Schnoodle's energy and allow him to do his business. Even if you have a fenced-in yard, it's still a good idea to walk him, as walking together is a great bonding experience for you and your Schnoodle.

Here are a few tips to maximize your Schnoodle's exercise time:

- Walk him for at least 20 to 30 minutes at a time.

- Choose a safe and comfortable surface for the Schnoodle to walk on. Make sure that the sidewalk or asphalt is not too hot or too cold, as this can damage paw pads. If you cannot walk him in soft grass when the asphalt is hot or cold, you can purchase special doggy booties to put on his feet, which will protect him. He might not like them very much, but they'll keep him safe!

- Always check the Schnoodle's paws and pads before and after your walk to ensure that they are not sore, cut or even bleeding.

- When walking on a leash, always keep your Schnoodle by your side. Never pull or tug sharply on the leash, as this can damage his esophagus.

Obesity in Schnoodles

It is not unusual for a Schnoodle to potentially become overweight. This can be a problem, as his weight will put pressure on his joints and can lead to tendon strain and loss of joint cartilage. Also, your Schnoodle's chance of organ failure, heart disease, and cancer increase when he gains excess weight.

It's crucial to understand how to keep his weight managed as well as how to spot the signs of an overweight dog.

How Can You Tell If Your Schnoodle Is Overweight?

A year ago, while volunteering at my local animal shelter, I was tending to an older Basset hound mix that had been brought in a few days prior. The little guy was dreadfully overweight; he had big rolls of fat up and down his back, and he could barely waddle around his pen. Another volunteer approached, and I began to speak of his condition and how awful I felt for him. She belligerently informed me that the Basset was not, in fact, overweight, but that all

Basset Hounds looked like that. She argued with me up and down, and it astounded me that she couldn't see how obese he was. But she was a young lady who didn't have much in the way of experience with dogs, and looking back on the incident I can hardly fault her for the mistake.

Some dogs, like the Basset Hound, are indeed built stockier than other breeds, making it harder for the untrained eye to detect the signs of obesity. However, no matter the breed of dog, there's a surefire way to tell if the dog is overweight or not. (Luckily the Schnoodle has a rather normal build, so it won't be easy to mistake your dog's extra body fat as his natural build.)

You can tell that your Schnoodle is overweight if you are unable to feel the dog's ribs or backbone on your own, without having to press down too hard.

Also, the waist on your dog should be easily visible. These should be a slight tucking look around the abdomen as well. If he does not have a visible waist, he is obese, and measures should be taken immediately to bring him down to a healthy weight.

How to Get Your Schnoodle to Lose Weight

There are a couple of things that you can do to help your Schnoodle shed pounds and return to a healthy body weight.

- Adjust the calories that you allow your dog to consume in a typical day. A small amount of fat is still needed to ensure that his skin and coat remain healthy, but you need to keep caloric and fat levels down. For best results, contact your veterinarian to work out a diet that would be best suited for his needs.

- Encourage your Schnoodle to be more active. Schedule a regular workout plan and allow him to get enough exercise in a typical day. Play fetch with him, chase him around the yard or take him to a dog park to play with other dogs. By incorporating fun into his workout, you can ensure that he'll drop off the weight easily and without much stress. (Just make sure you don't push him too hard at first; this can lead to fatigue or injury).

- Reduce any treats or snacks that you give him. In fact, in the beginning, it is probably best to cut them out altogether, and if you do give him treats, make sure they are low calorie and high in protein. A jerky-based treat is best.

Key Health Problems To Watch Out For

While Schnoodles are fantastic dogs that are generally healthy and robust, unfortunately, there are a couple of health issues that they are prone to. These conditions can be uncomfortable and potentially dangerous if left unchecked, and it's crucial to monitor his health and keep an eye out for any potential problems that may arise during his lifespan.

These health problems are prominent in both the Poodle and the Schnauzer, and unfortunately, Schnoodles are genetically predisposed to develop them. Fortunately, most of them can be treated by a veterinarian, and it's important to catch them early.

Skin Allergies

It is not unusual for some Schnoodles to have skin allergies. These allergies cause rashes and other forms of irritation on a dog's skin. Allergies can be difficult to predict and can arise at any time, seemingly without provocation.

Some signs of skin allergies are red splotches on the skin and excessive scratching.

Sometimes skin allergies might be triggered by chemicals in your dog's shampoo or any other substance he might have come in contact with. Other times they are caused by pollen or smog, or by ingredients in his food. This is especially common amongst dogs who are fed a low-quality diet.

You can treat the rashes with an over-the-counter skin cream or an oatmeal-based shampoo. If they reoccur, take him to the vet, who will discover the source of his allergies and advise you on how best to avoid the triggers in the future.

Ear Infections

Ear infections are common amongst Schnoodles, mostly due to the long hair around their ear canals which can trap bacteria. Ear infections are very painful and bothersome, and if left untreated can even lead to a short-term hearing loss.

To prevent ear infections, trim the hair around your

Schnoodle's ear canals frequently, and keep the ear clean by gently dabbing it with a moist cotton ball (do not use a cotton swab! This can damage the inside of his ear.) Ear cleaning will be more thoroughly discussed during the 'Grooming' chapter.

If you notice your Schnoodle frequently shaking his head and scratching at his ears, he might have an ear infection. There might also be redness in his ear canal. A vet will prescribe medicine, most likely medicated ear drops, which should clear it right up.

Seborrhea (Oily or Dry Skin Patches)

Seborrhea is a condition that causes the skin to develop red, itchy skin patches.

This condition can cause your Schnoodle to develop flaky skin, a condition also known as dandruff.

This condition can be either dry or oily. In most cases, your dog will develop a combination of these two at the same time. Seborrhea is very itchy and uncomfortable.

This condition can also cause a greasy substance to gather around the ears, around the elbows and ankles, and on the underbelly.

The worst part about seborrhea is that it is not a condition that can be easily treated. However, a good medicated shampoo provided to you by your vet can help. Your vet can figure out what might be useful for your dog by testing a sample on a small part of the dog's body.

While he's being treated, it's important to keep your Schnoodle hydrated.

Schnauzer Comedo Syndrome (Bumps on the Body)

Schnauzer Comedo Syndrome is a condition that is most common amongst Schnauzers, and therefore Schnoodles as well. This is an acne-like condition that will cause raised bumps to develop on your Schnoodle's skin.

Specifically, blackheads can start to develop on the dog's back. These blackheads will be easily visible and therefore easy to diagnose the condition. Schnauzer Comedo Syndrome can be prevented with proper grooming, as it is caused by an imbalance of oils in the dog's coat.

You can treat this condition by applying hydrogen peroxide to the bumps and rubbing it gently into your dog's coat.

Epilepsy (Seizures)

Epilepsy is a condition that commonly occurs in Poodles, and unfortunately, Schnoodles have inherited the tendency to develop it as well. Epilepsy is a brain disorder that causes the dog to have seizures. He will begin to shake violently and uncontrollably, and he may even lose consciousness. A typical seizure can last for about 30 to 90 seconds. The condition is not known to be deadly, but it can be extremely disruptive to the dog.

A medication prescribed by your vet may be required to control seizures.

Patellar Luxation (Slipping Kneecap)

A patellar luxation is a condition where the kneecap will slip. This is a serious problem that can cause your dog to be unable to move properly.

This condition, which can simply be referred to as kneecap dislocation, develops as the kneecap, or patella, is dislocated from the natural groove formed in the thigh bone.
This condition is more likely to be found in a Toy Schnoodle as smaller dogs tend to suffer from patellar luxation. Also, females are slightly more likely to develop this condition than males.

The condition is often genetic, and it's important to consult a breeder before you purchase a puppy from them to ensure that the puppy will not be genetically disposed to develop it later on. Extreme trauma, such as a car accident, may also cause a dislocation to take place.

A vet can identify kneecap dislocation via x-ray and may be treated through a surgical procedure. A surgical fastener may be installed within the joint to make it easier for the kneecap to stay in place in the future.

Canine Hyperlipidemia (High Cholesterol In the Blood)

Canine hyperlipidemia is a serious blood disorder that many Schnoodles might be at risk of developing. This is a condition where the dog's bloodstream will contain abnormally high cholesterol levels.

This condition often comes about as a result of an unhealthy diet. You will need to make sure you feed your Schnoodle a healthy, balanced diet and ensure that he gets plenty of exercise.

Hyperlipidemia can be difficult to identify without a proper blood test. However, signs of this disorder are sudden weight gain and fatigue.

A defect in proteins or enzymes within the body that carry and break down cholesterol deposits may also be a problem. This is a concern that many breeders are willing to try and control in the dogs that they are raising.

A vet can diagnose hyperlipidemia via a blood test. This condition can be treated with medications and exercise. Even after he's been cleared by the vet, it's still a good idea to get him frequently retested to ensure that the condition does not reappear.

Chapter 7 –Grooming Your Schnoodle

One of the things I adore most about Schnoodles is their thick, slightly curly coat! It is arguably one of their best features, a striking yet subtle distinction that certainly sets them apart from the crowd.

However, that coat does need a good bit of grooming, and you will have to spend some time caring for it. Grooming can be a lot of work; however, after some time the grooming process will seem more or less routine to you. Grooming is also a way for you to bond with your Schnoodle as well.

In this chapter, you'll find tips on how to care for your Schnoodle's unique coat as well as ear, nail, and eye care.

Grooming your Schnoodle's Unique Coat

The Schnoodle's coat is absolutely beautiful—soft and curly when cared for properly. It's up to you to keep it that way! In this section, we'll cover the basics of grooming.

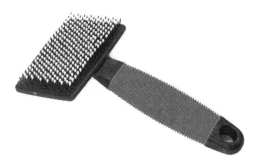

A good wire brush is a very important grooming tool that every Schnoodle owner must have. Just don't press too hard!

It is best to groom your Schnoodle after he's through walking or playing. It is easier for a dog to be receptive to a bath or other kind of grooming session if he is not too energetic.

Also, be sure to start grooming your Schnoodle as early as you can, while he's still a puppy if that's possible. Bathing and combing can be stressful to dogs if they aren't used to it at first, and by getting him accustomed early you can be sure that he'll grow to, if not love it, at least tolerate it!

Combing Your Schnoodle

Thankfully, the Schnoodle's coat is hypoallergenic and not prone to shedding, which means that, unlike many other long-haired breeds, you won't have to brush it every single day to cut down on shedding!

Still, you will need to comb your Schnoodle regularly. While it is true that it doesn't shed much, brushing will keep his skin healthy and his hair shiny.

You should comb him two to four times a week.

Make sure that you comb your Schnoodle's coat in the same direction. Use a good brush that has smooth bristles and will get into the coat without scratching the skin.

Here are some more tips that you should keep in mind while brushing your Schnoodle:

- Check around his coat for fleas or ticks.

- Use a flexible rubber brush that can move well through the coat.

- Check the bristles on your brush to ensure that they won't break apart.

Don't forget to use a comb that is specifically for dogs. A curved comb is always a good option. Also a wire brush as in the illustration above, just be careful not to press too hard into your Schnoodle's skin.

Bathing Your Schnoodle

A key part of your Schnoodle's grooming regimen is bathing. Regular baths will keep his coat soft, clean, and smelling great, and is also important to maintain skin health.

You should bathe your Schnoodle once a week; any more

than that and his skin might dry out and become flaky and itchy. Choose a high-quality doggy shampoo; I prefer shampoos that are oatmeal-based as they smell great and are terrific for dogs with sensitive skin or dogs that are prone to itchiness.

You can choose to bathe your Schnoodle either outside in a metal washing tub or inside in the bathtub. I prefer using the bathtub, but many dogs are too large or too skittish for that. If you have a Giant Schnoodle, outside bathing is recommended; otherwise, he's sure to make a mess!

Here're some things to keep in mind while bathing your Schnoodle:

- Use lukewarm water. Test the temperature with the inside of your wrist; if it burns, it's too hot.

- Always use a groomer-approved dog shampoo when washing your Schnoodle; don't use yours, no matter how good it might smell! A dog shampoo will be mild and won't contain any compounds that might be harsh on your dog's skin.

- Avoid getting suds or water into your Schnoodle's eyes, nose, or ears.

- Rinse his coat thoroughly, and after you're done, dry his coat with either a towel or a hair dryer set on the lowest setting. Gently comb out his coat once it's dry to remove any tangles.

- Many dogs get anxious during bath time. Pet him and speak to him in a soft, soothing voice to reassure him, and always give him a treat or his favorite toy afterward.

Trimming

A Schnoodle's coat is naturally long, but there are some spots on his body that you will need to keep trimmed on a regular basis. Use a pair of long, narrow trimming scissors to trim the hair around his eyes, ears, and genital regions to avoid soiling and matting.

Be very cautious when trimming your Schnoodle's hair. Be sure that you do this after washing and make sure that he remains calm.

Schnauzer and Poodle Mix Nail Care

Your Schnoodle's nails should be checked carefully to see that they are healthy. The nails must be easy for the dog to walk on so it will not suffer from any substantial pains while moving around.

You need to make sure the nails are trimmed on a weekly basis. If left unchecked, the nails will start to curl up and might impair his ability to walk.

Purchase a dog nail trimmer with a curved, angled design and an attached nail guard that will help prevent you from cutting off too much of the nail at a time. Examine your Schnoodle's nails and identify the 'quick,' which is a blood vessel that runs through the nail. Always be sure to cut above the quick; be careful not to cut it.

Always choose a stainless-steel nail clipper with a nail guard. Ask your veterinarian or groomer to recommend their favorite one!

Pad Care

You must check the pads on your Schnoodle's feet on a regular basis. This is especially since they can suffer from fatigue from walking on hard surfaces. The pads should not be cut, bruised, or bleeding. Also be sure to trim any excess hair around his toenails.

If your dog's pads are injured, keep him off of his feet for a while until they heal.

Eye Care

While I love the Schnoodle's curly coat, one problem commonly seen in this designer breed is hair that can grow over the Schnoodle's eyes, impairing his vision and trapping potentially harmful bacteria in his eyes. Eye care is just as important, if not more so than coat care.

Start by trimming the hair around the Schnoodle's eyes every week.

Like most dogs, Schnoodles are prone to tear stains on the coat around the eyes. Not only is this unsightly, but it can also attract bacteria to his eyes. Every day, take a cotton ball and dip it into warm water. Use it to gently clean around his eyes to get rid of eye discharge and keep the tear stains from setting in.

Check your dog's eyes regularly to see that they are clear. If you see any cloudy spots, fluid deposits, redness, or irritation, consult your veterinarian.

Ear Care

Trim the hair around your Schnoodle's ears every week. You must hold the hair from its end while you trim it so it will not fall into the ear canal.

Every few days, clean your Schnoodle's ears. If his ears aren't cleaned frequently, he runs the risk of developing an ear infection; as stated in the previous chapter, this particular mix is prone to ear infections. Therefore, you should always remain cautious and take preventative measures.

Dampen a cotton ball with clean water and then wipe off the outside area of the ears. Start with the outside flap; you might have to replace the cotton ball a few times.

Next, you must work a little deeper into the ears. You should move into the ears to clean out the wax, dust, and dirt that may have accumulated there.

Only wash what you can see! Do not go into his ear canal, as this can damage his eardrum and cause potentially permanent injury.

All in all, grooming might be a time-consuming process, but it's worth it to keep your Schnoodle clean and healthy.

Chapter 8 – Schnoodle Training – How Does It Work?

As you read earlier, the Schnoodle is a dog that is bred from two of the world's smartest dog breeds. With that in mind, it is no surprise that the Schnoodle is relatively easy to train!

However, you still must have a detailed plan in hand. You have to remain control of the situation, no matter how frustrating it gets, particularly if this is your first time training a dog. Schnoodles are extremely smart, but many of them, particularly the larger Schnoodles, tend to possess a stubborn streak. Remain calm, firm, and consistent in your training, and before too long you'll have the bragging rights to a perfectly trained Schnoodle!

The best part of training your Schnoodle is that you'll spend plenty of time with him. One of the wonderful things about dogs, especially gentle ones like the Schnoodle, is that they are very eager to please their human family members. After a while, you'll find that your Schnoodle will work very hard in his training simply to make you happy. Always be sure to praise him when he does something right.

Obedience Training

If your Schnoodle likes to chew up your shoes, refuses to behave on a leash, or just doesn't listen to you, obedience training is definitely the way to go! Obedience training is a good idea anyway, and you should research proper training methods before you bring home a Schnoodle puppy.

Always put your best foot forward when it comes to your

Schnoodle's training. If you're bored, he'll pick up on your mood and quickly lose interest.

The process of obedience training is a rather simple one. It involves working with sensible commands through a few steps.

Sitting

You can get a Schnoodle to learn to sit on command by getting down to the dog's level. As you do this, hold a treat near his nose and let the dog's head follow as you move it upward.

Schnoodles are bright dogs that are always eager to please their owners, which makes them very easy to train!

After this, look to see that the dog's rear end lowers down.

This should show that the dog is ready to sit. When he does sit, give him that treat and praise him for his effort.

Be sure to repeat this a few times in a day and pair the action with the word "sit." This allows your Schnoodle to associate the command with the reward.

Coming To You

You can get your Schnoodle to come to you by your command as well. To do this, you must clip a collar and a leash on him, and then have him follow you around a yard.

Once it's fresh in his brain that he's to come to you, unclip the leash, but first, make sure you're first in a dog-safe area, and walk a good distance away from him. Then crouch down, say 'Come' and hold out a treat.

When he comes to you, praise him and give him the treat. Be sure you pair the action with the proper trigger word so the dog will associate that word with the command.

Staying In Place

To get your Schnoodle to stay in place, first, you must have him in front of you, preferably sitting.

Wave your palm in front of the dog's nose. Use a command like "stay" to bring your point across.

Step back, and then step back more if he stays. Reward your Schnoodle only when he stays in its place. If he moves, put the dog back in his initial place and repeat the action. This can be done several times a day in many locations around the house.

These methods for training your Schnoodle have proven to be effective. If you follow them, your Schnoodle will learn to avoid improper behaviors and will start to listen to you. Just remember to stay consistent! Dogs like routine, remember? Remember to never, ever scold your Schnoodle when he doesn't understand what you want him to do right away. It will only confuse him and bring down his morale, which will negatively affect his training.

Bathroom and House Training

You will need to make sure that your Schnoodle is properly trained for when he has to relieve himself. The last thing you want is for your Schnoodle to have frequent accidents in the house!

Fortunately, it's quite easy to housetrain dogs, particularly intelligent ones like Schnoodles; they don't like having excrement in their living spaces any more than we do.

How Can You Identify When He Needs to Go?

You can tell that your Schnoodle needs to go to the bathroom if he circles, sniffing the floor and acting anxious, nervous, or restless. He may shake, which means that he is holding his bowels.

It's important to set up a bathroom schedule for your Schnoodle. He will, of course, need to relieve himself when he wakes up in the morning, just like people do, and then again around midday and once more at night before he goes to bed.

Preparing a Space To Go

If you have a smaller Schnoodle and don't have the time or means to take him outside, you can train him to use a puppy pad or a newspaper. Simply place him on the newspaper when you know he has to use the bathroom and don't allow him to get off of it until he urinates or defecates. It may take several tries for him to get the hang of it; for best results place the pad or newspaper near the front door; he will know that he's supposed to go outside to use the bathroom and will instead use it on the paper when he knows he can't hold it anymore. If you want to take it a step forward, shut your Schnoodle in the bathroom with the paper on the floor when he first wakes up in the morning. He will have no choice but to use the paper. After a few days, he'll catch on.

For larger dogs that can't use puppy pads or papers, or if that method is unappealing to you, lead your dog outside and find a safe spot for him to use the bathroom. Obviously, you will need to make sure it's a spot that is relatively private and will be far from plants, patio areas and other spots that people might often be around.

When you do identify that the Schnoodle needs to go to the bathroom, lead him to the space that you have designated. Make sure he fully relieves himself in that spot.

The above method is for people that cannot walk their dogs; I find it easier to simply walk them and allow them to use the bathroom where they want (keeping clear of yards and always picking up after them, of course).

What If My Schnoodle Has An Accident?

Unfortunately, there is always the chance that your dog might have an accident in the house. It's never fun to clean up a dog's mess. However, you must never scold him if he has an accident. If you do this, you might frighten him, and it might make it harder for him to use the bathroom where he's supposed to. Don't encourage or praise him, of course, but be gentle with him.

Crate or Bed Training

You can train your Schnoodle to stay in either a pet bed or a doggy crate; this is particularly useful if you want him to remain quiet, go to sleep, or restrict him from a certain area of the house for a short amount of time. Also, traveling with your Schnoodle will be much easier if he is already trained to sit quietly in a crate.

If you're training him to stay in a crate, always make sure it's comfortable for him. Place a pillow, some blankets, or a pet bed inside the crate and make sure it's large enough for him to move around comfortably in.

Bed or crate training can work well by simply leading your Schnoodle to the area when it's time to sleep. He might bark and whine at first, especially if you shut him in the crate, but after a while, he will calm down and even grow to enjoy it; dogs like a quiet place to go to unwind and relax just as much as people do.

Other Forms of Training

There are many other kinds of training that you can consider offering to your dog:

- You can train your dog to grab the newspaper in the morning and bring it to your doorstep.
- You can train the Schnoodle to learn how to stay quiet and to stop barking.
- You can even train it to learn how to respond to people and to come over to you when asked. This is for cases where the Schnoodle might be a little too interested in sniffing someone.

The principles for training your dog are essentially the same all around; show him an example of what you want him to do, use positive reinforcement such as praise and treats, and repeat until he understands.

Chapter 9 –Vaccinating Your Schnoodle

Now, in earlier chapters we covered the principles of general Schnoodle health and what problems you can expect; in the next couple of chapters we will discuss the more in-depth, and ultimately more important, health issues.

Like with any other dog breed, your Schnoodle will require regular vaccinations to prevent many potentially life-threatening diseases and illnesses.

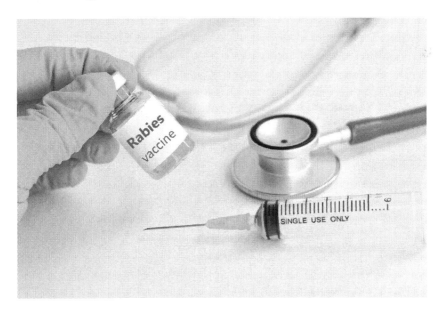

Getting a shot might hurt a little bit, but vaccinations are crucial to the long-term health of your Schnoodle.

You will have to talk with your veterinarian about a proper schedule for how these vaccinations are to be administered. If you choose to purchase your Schnoodle from a breeder, it's also an excellent idea to ask the breeder about the vaccinations that the puppy has already received.

A Listing of the Key Injections

There are several illnesses that your Schnoodle must be vaccinated against.

- An annual **rabies** shot is needed to protect the Schnoodle from this deadly virus. Rabies is spread through saliva and, if your dog is not vaccinated against it, can be transmitted through a bite by stray or wild animals that carry the virus. Rabies is extremely deadly; there's no cure for it, and if your dog contracts rabies, he will have to be put down.

- **Distemper** is a viral disease that will cause heavy coughing and a high fever. Distemper can be fatal to your Schnoodle if he's not protected against it; a yearly vaccine is highly recommended.

- **Parvovirus** is a virus that attacks the cells in a dog's body. This will weaken his condition greatly and is fatal if not treated. Your dog will need a parvovirus vaccination every year.

- **Hepatitis** is a dangerous condition in which the liver becomes infected. This makes it harder for the dog to properly process toxins and clean his blood, leading to sickness and possibly death. Your veterinarian can recommend a hepatitis vaccination schedule for your Schnoodle.

- **Leptospirosis** is a condition that causes urinary tract infection. This disease can be spread through the urine. It can cause severe kidney damage if not treated properly, so you must get a vaccination for this every three years.

- **Parainfluenza** is similar to the common flu that people can suffer from but it can be even more harmful to a dog, and possibly even deadly. This can cause severe respiratory damages and can weaken the dog's ability to breathe properly. An annual parainfluenza vaccination is needed.

- **Kennel cough** is a respiratory disease that may be caused by improper living conditions, as bacteria can move into the lungs and airways, thus causing breathing issues. Kennel cough vaccinations aren't nearly as vital as vaccinations against the deadlier diseases, but your vet may still recommend adding it to your Schnoodle's vaccinations.

- A **coronavirus** vaccination is needed at about ten to twelve weeks of age. Coronavirus is a bacterial condition that weakens the lungs and causes shortness of breath.

What's the Best Schedule?

Your vet will set up a vaccination schedule for your Schnoodle depending on his age, health, and what vaccinations he's received before. However, this is a typical dog vaccination schedule:

- Distemper, hepatitis, parvovirus, and parainfluenza injections are needed at 6 to 8 weeks of age.

- These must be repeated at 10 to 12 weeks with the leptospirosis vaccine added. A coronavirus vaccination is also needed alongside a kennel cough vaccine.

- The first four vaccines listed are to be repeated at 14 to 16 weeks.

- The first four have to be used alongside a rabies vaccine and a hepatitis shot every year.

- The leptospirosis vaccine is needed every three years and can be administered alongside the other vaccines listed.

Always stick to your vet's recommended schedule and never miss an appointment. In many cases, vaccines are all that stand between your dog and a serious disease, and vaccines are a vital part of your Schnoodle's health, safety, and wellbeing.

Chapter 10 – Internal And External Parasites

Like all dogs, Schnoodles are vulnerable to all sorts of parasites such as ticks, fleas, and worms. Parasites are incredibly irritating and, in extreme cases, can cause diseases or even death.

It's highly likely, and some would say even unavoidable, that at least at one point of time your Schnoodle will carry at least one type of parasite. Therefore, I've dedicated this chapter to the different sort of pests that your Schnoodle might come into contact with, the diseases they might carry, the risks they pose to your dog's health, and ways to prevent and control them.

External Pest Control

Pests like fleas and ticks can be harmful to your Schnoodle. Fleas are tiny little insects that pierce the skin and drink the dog's blood. They multiply extremely rapidly and if left unchecked can quickly infest a dog, especially a long-haired dog like the Schnoodle. Their bites cause intense itching and even pain if the fleas are numerous enough, and your Schnoodle may scratch himself hard enough to break the skin.

Ticks, while usually not as numerous as fleas, are just as bad if not worse; they burrow into the dog's skin and latch on, drinking blood until they swell up to several times their normal size. They prefer the skin around the dog's ears, shoulders, and hindquarters, but will latch anywhere they can. Ticks are markedly more dangerous than fleas, as they tend to carry serious diseases such as Lyme disease and yellow fever. They are also harder to remove from your dog's body.

There are many things that can be done to keep pests off of your Schnoodle:

- While it is important to bring him outside for walks and exercise, make sure you try and keep him indoors when he's not exercising to minimize the risk of picking up any outside pests.

- Wash and groom your Schnoodle regularly.

- You can treat your lawn with pesticides that will kill fleas and ticks.

- Treat your Schnoodle with a vet-approved flea-and-tick preventative topical or oral medicine, or purchase a flea collar.

What Do You Do When There's A Tick On Your Schnoodle?

The worst part about ticks is that they are notorious for burrowing into a dog's skin and sticking there, making it extremely hard to remove safely.

As easy as it can be, do not simply pull the tick out. There's always the chance that the tick's proboscis, the narrow part of its mouth that it uses to drink the blood, can remain embedded in your dog's skin, which can cause infection. It can also further damage your Schnoodle's skin and leave a gaping wound.

Instead, use any of the following methods to remove ticks:

- Your vet can provide you with a treatment that you can apply directly to the tick.

- There are some over-the-counter dog shampoos available for purchase at most pet supply stores that kill both fleas and ticks.

- A tick dip is a solution that can be diluted with water and then applied onto the impacted area. This can kill ticks very well, but you must make sure it is diluted first and that you don't use it on a dog that is too young, is pregnant, or is nursing.

Worms and Heartworms

Worms can pose a serious threat to any dog, including Schnoodles. Worms, including heartworms, are internal parasites; that is, they attack the inside of your dog's body instead of the outside.

Worms are usually transmitted through the bite of a mosquito that has been bitten an animal that is already infested with worms. The worm's eggs travel through the bloodstream of an infected animal, and into the mosquito, which then transmits the eggs when it bites another animal, such as your poor Schnoodle.

Over the course of six months or so, the eggs hatch and form into fully-grown worms, which then take up residence in your dog's organs, like his intestines.

Worms can cause all sorts of horrible problems. Some species of worms only take nutrition from the food that dogs ingest; others eat away at the dog's body.

In the case of heartworms, the dog's blood vessels will start to weaken and narrow, due to the inflammation that the heartworms trigger around the blood vessels. Treatment for heartworms is a long, arduous, and expensive process, and it's best to prevent these parasites rather than treat them.

Most forms of internal parasites are extremely hard to detect, meaning that in many cases a dog might be infested, and you wouldn't even know it.

How Can You Identify Worms?

If you suspect that your Schnoodle is suffering from a worm infestation, bring him to the veterinarian immediately to set up a treatment plan. A dog infested with worms might exhibit any of the following symptoms:

- Frequent vomiting.

- Persistent, harsh coughing.

- Swelling in the midsection.

- Rapid weight loss.

- Worm segments lodged in feces.

How Can You Treat Worms and Heartworms?

There are several different treatment options available for worms.

- For most intestinal worms, your vet might recommend and over-the-counter oral medication that will kill the worms.

- Your vet may prescribe a melarsomine injection. This is a drug that is known to treat many infections, particularly heartworm infections. It can be a long process, but if your Schnoodle is treated early enough, it should be successful.

- Your vet may also recommend a long-term worm preventative medicine to help keep your Schnoodle healthy while also preventing any potential re-infestations in the future.

Virtually any medical condition can be treated, but remember, prevention is the absolute best option when it comes to protecting your precious Schnoodle's health!

Chapter 11 – Schnoodle Breeding

There comes a time in many dog owners' lives that they may decide to breed their beloved pets. You might decide to breed your Schnoodle for many different reasons; to create a supplemental income, to increase your dog's worth in the eyes of breeders, or simply for the joy of bringing new, adorable Schnoodle puppies into the world for the public to enjoy.

Many people who are new to the world of canine breeding decide to breed their dogs for one reason only—money. If this is your sole motivation, I must advise a word of caution. Unless you are well established in the industry, you probably won't make a lot of money at first. Dog breeding is an in-depth process that requires a lot of time and money before you can even get started. Unfortunately, this is the reason that so many unscrupulous and irresponsible breeders exist; they are not willing to put forth the money and effort needed to ensure safe, responsible breeding.

Always practice safe, responsible breeding!

If you choose to breed your Schnoodle, start small. If you have a female Schnoodle, you should purchase a healthy young intact male from a good bloodline; you can check with other Schnoodle breeders to see if such a dog is available. A cheaper option would be to find a stud dog; for a fee of either cash or the first pick of the litter, the owner of a stud dog will lend the stud to you for the breeding process.

Dog breeding, especially for such an obscure designer breed such as the Schnoodle, can be a challenge. It isn't quite as straightforward as simply breeding and selling puppies; you alone are responsible for the health, temperament, safety, and wellbeing of both the mother and her puppies.

In this chapter, we will discuss the mechanics of breeding Schnoodles, how to care for a nursing mother and her litter, the birthing process, and what you should expect during each stage.

Giant Schnoodle Puppies, Toy Schnoodles Puppies, and More – Litter Size

Before you make the decision to breed your Schnoodle, it's a good idea to research the breed and develop an understanding of what to expect. Litter production and the number of puppies born in each litter vary from breed to breed.

A typical Schnoodle litter will consist of two to six dogs, with four or five being most common. On rare occasions, a single pup will be born, and smaller litters are typical amongst Toy Schnoodles.

There are a few factors which may contribute to the size of your Schnoodle's litter.

- An older mother will have fewer puppies in a litter on average.

- A larger breed variation, such as the Giant Schnoodle, will typically produce more puppies in a litter as opposed to smaller dogs.

- A first-time mother will usually produce fewer puppies as well.

It might be possible you to feel the mother's body halfway during a typical 58 to 68-day pregnancy to get an idea of precisely how many puppies she will produce. For a more accurate way to determine litter size, take the mother to the vet for an ultrasound; this is a good idea anyway, as it's important to evaluate the health of the puppies.

The Mother's Health

No matter what your reason for breeding your Schnoodle, it's fundamental that you put the female Schnoodle's health and comfort first. Not only will this ensure a smoother process, but it's also the right thing to do.

The mother's health will have a profound impact on the litter itself; a healthy dog will produce healthy puppies.

Before you begin the breeding process, please keep the following points in mind:

- Always wait until the mother is at least a year and a half to two years old before she is bred; or rather after she's experienced two complete heat cycles. Female dogs usually first go into heat when they're six to eight months old, then every six months to a year afterward. Breed her on her third heat for best results.
- Allow the mother about a year's time in between litters. This is to not only allow her to have time with her puppies and to take care of them in their earliest months but also to ensure that her body can recover from the strain of giving birth and nursing.

- A Schnoodle mother must also be removed from any breeding lines if the puppies she has produced have proven to have substantial medical issues. This is to ensure that she does not put the gene pool at any more risk.

Schnoodle Pregnancy

After the mating, be sure to take your Schnoodle to the veterinarian to receive confirmation that the breeding was successful. Once you're sure that your Schnoodle is indeed pregnant, it's crucial to monitor her pregnancy every step of the way to ensure that the puppies are healthy.

Keep her inside and only let her out for short walks, especially later in her pregnancy. Make sure she always has access to clean drinking water and as much food as she wants; she alone knows her body and knows how much her growing puppies need. Pregnant dogs will double their food intake.

Make sure that she stays off of furniture where she might fall or jump, especially if she is a Miniature Schnoodle. Of course, you wouldn't want her to get hurt anyway, but she might also inadvertently injure her unborn puppies as well.

Keep your veterinarian on speed-dial! If a problem or concern arises, don't hesitate to call him. Prepare yourself for frequent vet visits for ultrasounds, bloodwork, and just general checkups to ensure that the pregnancy is going smoothly.

Pregnancy in dogs lasts approximately 63 days, give or take a few days. Smaller breeds tend to go into labor a week or so sooner than larger dogs, but this is by no means a sure thing; make sure you're ready for the birth well before the 63-day mark just to be safe.

When the due date approaches, your Schnoodle's teats will swell and become very prominent. You might be able to feel the puppies by gently laying a hand on her abdomen; when you feel them move around, you will know that she will deliver soon. She may become either very lazy or very restless and her food intake will increase steadily.

A day or so before labor, your Schnoodle may show restless behavior such as pacing, panting, or whining. Many dogs refuse food and will only drink water. She will begin to look for a place to 'nest'; that is, a place that's well out of the way of the main hustle and bustle of the house, a place where she can safely curl up and deliver her puppies.

About twenty years ago I was fostering a young pregnant Labrador. She went into labor a few days earlier than I expected, and with me being young and foolish I didn't think to make preparations in advance. I paid dearly for my lack of foresight; to put a long story short, I came home from the grocery store and found that the dog in question had begun to give birth in my closet, practically right on top of my shoes! I don't need to say that it was a highly unpleasant experience, and never again in all my years have I failed to prepare for a dog's pregnancy in advance.

Forgive my long-windedness—my point is, at least two weeks before the expected due date, prepare a whelping box for your pregnant Schnoodle. A whelping box is a large cardboard or wooden box lined with soft towels or old blankets. Make sure that she can easily climb in and out of it, and place the box in a quiet, secluded place; perhaps in a closet or behind some furniture, where she won't be disturbed. Show her the box several times in the days before her labor, and when she sits down in it praise her. Most likely she will use it when she goes into labor, but just to be safe discourage her from using any other place in the house. Close all doors, especially to closets, and make sure there are no enclosed spaces that she might slip into.

Once she goes into labor, she will retreat to her whelping box. Now, there are two schools of thought as to what you, as her owner, should do next. Some people think that you should simply leave them alone; labor is a painful and stressful time for the mother dog, and she might prefer to be left to her own devices. 98 percent of canine labors go smoothly with no human interference, and you are by no means obligated to watch over her; however, if you wish you might stay with her during the birthing process, both to reassure her and to be present in case there are any difficulties. If she is a first-time mother I strongly recommend staying by her side; she might be frightened, and your presence alone can do wonders for her morale. There's not much you can do, unfortunately, but pet her and speak to her in a calm, soothing voice. Be prepared, however, as the full birthing process from start to finish can be a long one.

The puppies will come one at a time, and she will clean them and break the amniotic sac and the umbilical cord. If she doesn't break the umbilical cords, cut them yourself with a pair of sanitized steel scissors.

Once all of the puppies have been born, she will push out the placenta. Afterward, she will relax and nurse her puppies. Be sure to exercise caution; many mother dogs are protective of their newborn puppies and depending on her personality and the level of her pain, she might snap at you. As soon as you're certain that she and the puppies are okay, leave her alone for a while. Be sure to place some food and water near the whelping box.

The Growth of Schnoodle Puppies

The puppies will grow extremely quickly. They're blind at birth but after a couple of weeks will open their eyes, and after three to four weeks they will be able to walk. When they're four weeks old, they should be weaned. The weaning process is fairly simple; provide the puppies with either canned food or some dry dog food that is specially formulated for puppies with a little warm water or milk mixed in. They will nibble at the food at first, but in a matter of days will make the transition from their mother's milk to solid food.

By this time the puppies will be very playful! Be sure to provide them with plenty of toys; bored puppies can and will destroy your shoes and furniture.

At eight to ten weeks of age, your Schnoodle puppies will be able to leave their mother. Even before they're old enough to be sold, make sure that the people interested in buying the puppies can provide them with a safe, loving home. Ask plenty of questions and don't sell your puppies to just anybody. So many dogs wind up in animal shelters or, worse, abandoned on the streets for this reason: many people want a puppy but aren't willing to put forth the time and effort it takes to take care of them or do not want the dog anymore after it's no longer tiny and adorable. You can avoid such a fate for your Schnoodle's puppies by making sure that they go to a family that will love and cherish them for the rest of their days.

Conclusion

All in all, the Schnoodle is a wonderful, amazing, beautiful dog that is just bursting with love to give. This unique dog is intelligent and friendly and is sure to bring you and your family nothing but the upmost delight.

Designer breeds may be a relatively new addition to the canine world, but I am fully confident that the Schnoodle is here to stay for good.

You'd truly be hard-pressed to find a cuter, more loving companion!

As long as you make sure to feed your Schnoodle a healthy diet, groom him regularly, train him, and give him every bit of love and affection that he deserves, your Schnoodle will thrive!

Schnoodles are one of the most unique dog mixes in the world, and they've thoroughly won over my heart over the years. It is my sincerest hope that they will do the same to you.

Thank you very much for reading this book; I hope it was informative, and if I've convinced you to allow one of these beautiful, unique dogs a special place in your heart and home, I can consider my job well done.

A

B

C

immune system · 56, 66
industry · 39, 40, 100
infections · 16, 71, 82, 99
inflammation · 98
ingredients · 52, 53, 71
injury · 70, 83
intelligence · 9, 43, 44, 45, 47
intelligent · 9, 14, 19, 43, 44, 46, 49, 87, 109
itchiness · 79

J

joints · 68

K

kennel club · 8
kennel clubs · 21
kennel cough · 93, 94
kidney · 93
kneecap · 74

L

labor · 105, 106
Labradoodle · 8
leash · 66, 68, 84, 86
Leptospirosis · 93
life expectancy · 65
litter · 16, 30, 37, 102, 103
liver · 56, 60, 92

M

mating · 104
meat · 59, 60
medicine · 72, 96, 99
metabolic rates · 66
milk · 54, 55, 107
minerals · 52

Made in the USA
Lexington, KY
17 July 2019